moments of

gratitude

for
Black Women

A FAITH BASED JOURNAL

mbrace Gratitude. Deepen Your Faith. Transform Your Life.

moments of *gratitude*

for Black Women

A FAITH BASED JOURNAL ✝

Embrace Gratitude. Deepen Your Faith. Transform Your Life.

Alease Iyabo Fapohunda Warren

This journal is designed for Black women as a tool for personal reflection and empowerment. It is not intended to serve as a diagnostic tool or substitute for professional mental health care. The content provided is for informational and self-reflective purposes only. The views expressed in this journal are those of the author's and do not necessarily reflect the views of the publishers or editors. Consult with your physician prior to adopting any suggestions in this journal. If you require diagnosis or medical attention please seek support of a licensed mental health professional.

ABOUT THE
Author

Alease Warren is a licensed Social Worker and Mental Health Therapist who focuses on making space for Black women to feel supported, healed, and whole. She partners with women who struggle with depression, anxiety, trauma, and burnout, using a mixture of mindfulness, evidenced-based care, and biblical principles.

Alease is also the founder of **Iyabo's Treasure**, a movement created to cherish the legacy and joy of Black women. The name *Iyabo* was given to her by her father which was to honor his mother who passed away early in his life. Iyabo means "Mother has returned", or "Joy has returned" in Yoruba. For Alease, this name is both a tribute and a calling, symbolizing that healing is generational.

She is the creator of **The Power of Gratitude Journaling Workshop** which is an interactive experience that blends writing, reflection, and mindfulness to help women recharge.

As a therapist, she is trained in evidence-based practices such as Cognitive Behavioral Therapy, Cognitive Processing Therapy to treat long standing trauma, Motivational Interviewing, Dialectical Behavioral Therapy, and Solution-Focused Brief Therapy. Her approach to therapy is strengths-based and she helps you focus on internal strengths and resourcefulness. She is a member of the National Association of Christian Social Workers, and the National Association of Black Social Workers in the D.C. Metro Chapter.

To stay connected and explore more self-care and gratitude-centered content, you can follow her on Instagram, Pinterest, or Eventbrite: **@IyabosTreasure**.

Acknowledgements

I am grateful to God, who is my Rock and my Source.

To my husband, M'tchaka — thank you for being my greatest encourager and unwavering supporter.

To my bonus daughter, Noá — never forget how deeply I love you.

To my father, Abayomi (may he rest in peace), my mother Alexis (may she rest in peace), and my bonus mother, Comfort — thank you for your prayers, your unconditional love, and your constant support.

To my mother-in-law, Sheila — I am grateful for your mentorship, wisdom, and the steady guidance you offered as I brought this project to life.

To my best friends — Natasha and Tiffany— my soul sisters, my shoulders when I needed to lean, cry, or laugh. Thank you for holding space for me over and over again.

And last, but most definitely not least — to my siblings, Sabrina, Abiola, Subuola, Junior
Olamide, and Mojisola — may this journal empower you to continue your journey of loving yourselves deeply and loving others well.

"The Lord hath done great things for us; whereof we are glad." — Psalms 126:3 (NKJV)

Preface

This book is for women who need a safe space to rest, heal, and reconnect with God.

Let me tell you about my mother because she is the reason why this journal is here.

My mother was my pride and joy. Beautiful inside and out. With a smile like CeCe Winans, a body like Jill Scott, and a voice like Jennifer Holliday! Whew chile'…she was bad! She was the kind of woman whose presence lit up a room. When she **sangg** (not sing y'all, *LOL*), you felt it deep down in your soul! And when she smiled—everything around you became beautiful. Everybody who really knew her, knows what I am talking about!

My mother was one of the strongest women that I have ever known. Her story is sacred. I tell it as I experienced it. As her daughter. Not as a therapist. I honor my mother's light. At the same time I acknowledge the pain that so many Black women face. And my hope is that this story offers hope for healing where systems have failed us.

My mother has faced more than most people can imagine, on so many levels. But like many of us do, she silently carried her pain. Some of her battles were seen but many were not. And unfortunately as Black women, this is often the case in our community. Far too many of us go through battles alone, unseen, and on our own.

In the prime of her life, she faced serious health conditions that made it hard for her to have peace and enjoy her life. She fought to get help, but like a lot of Black women who entered the mental health system in the 1980s, she was let down by a system that was not built for her.

Even though a lot of efforts have been made to improve the healthcare systems in this country, these systems still do not serve our community on a level that is equitable. **But they were never designed to serve women of color!** And unfortunately, many families in our community do not have the resources to help their loved ones through what they are facing.

Sadly, this is a problem that is still here today. Racism is rooted in this country's healthcare structures. A lot of us do not get screened properly or sometimes, we feel like we are being dismissed or misunderstood. This only deepens the shame and stigma that is connected to mental health.

But the burden of this pain does not just live in the larger system. The racism and bias in healthcare, limited access to culturally affirming care, and the historical medical exploitation and distrust are not old stories from the past or ideas that are out there floating around.

No—these things are affecting our daily lives and the people we care about. This is personal. And we see it affecting our mothers, our sisters, our friends, and loved ones. You may even feel it in yourself. This is real and can run deep. But a lot of us have learned to hide it and go through life while the world looks past us.

It is time to change that.

Because you were never meant to carry it all by yourself. That is why this book was created. This is a space to process your emotions in a way that affirms you.

Almost 10 years have passed since my mother died. She was more than what she battled. She was Light. She was Beauty. She was Love. And I still carry her love in my heart and the lessons from her life. My passion for this book comes from seeing up close the damage that happens when we do not or cannot refill our cup. I have seen how it can affect us mentally, physically and emotionally when we are not able to process our emotions. It inspired me to write this journal. And it is here for you to explore, release, process, and replenish. Because I found that healing does not only come from the external systems that are around us—it actually can start from within.

The Power of Gratitude

I want to share a personal story with you. I remember one Sunday morning when I went to a worship service at a local church. During the service, a young lady got up to sing. But first, she said something that both nourished and challenged me. She said, "You cannot be depressed and grateful at the same time."

Now, I know our mental health has more layers than that. But back then, I remember looking up to her like *Forreal?* Could that be true for me? And so out of curiosity, I started practicing gratitude. I was not doing it to act like my pain did not exist- I was doing it to shift my focus. That was when something began to change.

It was hard at first, but I started with baby steps. I spent time writing in my journal - remembering how my mother used to sing to God, and thanking God for giving me strength to make it through the day.

Little by little, I felt a shift. The grief I had been carrying did not automatically go away, but it felt like the air around me was lifting Even today as a professional in the mental health field, I still turn to gratitude as a self-care practice. Gratitude journaling helps to slow us down. It refocuses our thoughts. It brings more peace. It is relaxing.

If you are struggling with feelings of anxiety or depression, I wrote this journal for you. I know how overwhelming that can be. But with the help of this journal, you can find a beautiful moment to treasure. The activities that you find in this book are here to help you rest, reflect, and reset. Feel free to write down where you see a blessing showing up in your life. Talk about how that particular blessing is making you feel. And then explore why it is standing out to you at this moment.

Sistahs Wellness Check

It is so important for us to check in with ourselves. Before you start writing, go to the Sistahs Wellness Check on page 16 to reflect on how you are feeling right now. The Sistahs Wellness Check is a mood chart with graphics and language that we relate to. It will help you label your feelings in a way that is authentic and real.

For more details, go to the *How to Use This Journal* section before starting the prompts. As you hold this journal in your hands, let it be a sanctuary for you. Let it help you rest. Let it help you reconnect with God. With yourself. Healing is a process, but you do not have to do it alone. Let us do it together.

TABLE OF CONTENTS

JOURNAL PAGE TOPICS

The Basics

How to Use this Journal

The Gratitude Self Care Assessment

This is a brief assessment that consists of 10 questions that will help to provide you with more insight into how often you notice your blessings and practice gratefulness. To kick off your journey, complete the assessment and use your scores to help clarify your goals for enhancing your gratitude as a self care practice.

Sistahs Wellness Check

Sis, you must know where you are, before you can chart out where you are going. Check in with your emotions at the start of your journey. Then come back to the **Sistahs Wellness Check** from time to time.

Reflective Prompt Questions

These are journal prompts that will help you to identify, explore, and become more aware of the many blessings in your life, in ways you may not have considered.

Activities

Throughout the journal are activities. Each activity is a unique reflective way to get you in the habit of practicing gratitude. Use this as an opportunity to decompress, and as a creative outlet to emotionally process.

Inspirational Quotes

Throughout are quotes and affirmations that will provide you with a moment of reflection and inspiration as you journal.

Tip: While you journal, have your favorite beverage, light a candle, sit in your favorite space, and create a vibe. Find a consistent area where you feel comfortable. Then let it flow.

About Gratitude

What Is Gratitude?

Saying "thank you" is *nice*, but being grateful is *better*.

Gratefulness is about making time to stop, think, and really take in all the good in your life. Webster's[1] Dictionary tells us that; *'Gratitude is the state of being grateful: thankfulness'*. But it is more than a state—this is a way to **heal**. It can change how you think and feel about yourself. How you think about your relationships. Even how you handle the ups and downs of life. Especially if you do it all the time.

The Difference Between Thankfulness & Gratitude

Dr. Joy Harden-Bradford[2], a licensed psychologist and the founder of Therapy for Black Girls, tells us the difference between just saying 'thank you' and gratitude:

"You see, there is a difference between being thankful and being grateful. When we are thankful, we are just consciously aware of another person's actions. So if someone allows you to cut in front of them while you are reading this … you are merely exercising polite behavior by thanking them. But being grateful and expressing gratitude *involves reflection and is a purposeful practice*."

Gratitude is when you start being more aware of your blessings in a way that goes beyond the surface. It changes the way you think. The choices you make. Even how you move in the world. I have to be honest—sometimes being grateful is not easy to do. Especially when things are really painful. It can be hard to see any beauty in life when we are hurt, disappointed, or stressed out. But that is when it has the most power to change everything. I know because I've embraced this journey.

Gratitude & Limitless Love

I want you to know that no matter where you are, love is limitless. Love is greater than anything you can think of. Love is greater than time, distance, past mistakes, or even death. Being grateful has a way of making room for love to stretch. It lets us know that the things that we thought were lost, were never truly lost. So today, I invite you to choose gratitude. Let it help unlock the door to healing in your life. Watch it even stretch across generations.

We have a saying in Yoruba that goes like this: **"A river that forgets its source will dry up."** Sometimes life can feel dry. But when we feel worn out and empty, a grateful heart can help to nourish us. It can help to make our lives beautiful again.

My Sister, maybe you are feeling dryness in your life right now. If so, I just want to say that you are not alone. You are not forgotten.

How Gratitude Can Heal Relationships

I want to share an example of how gratitude played a role in my personal journey of restoring a very important relationship— my relationship with my father. I share this as his daughter, not as a clinician. This is to show how gratitude shaped my own healing.

Healing does not always look the same for everyone, and that is okay. But my prayer is that my story brings hope and inspiration to you as you read along.

My father was a brave, loving, generous, kind, compassionate, and humble man of God. He was a blessing to so many people. Even today his name lives on as a pillar in the community here in the U.S. and even abroad. And it still tickles me to hear people say he was my twin, but it is true because we looked so much alike!

But for me as a child, his absence was hard to process. That unanswered question stayed with me emotionally for a long time.

The thing is— **sometimes things happen that we cannot control, and that do not always allow people to be where they want to be.** Life is complex that way. But when we open our hearts to God through gratitude, we can start to see how love can stretch. We see it stretch across time and distances. And even in things unsaid. Gratefulness has been the thing that has helped me to experience the fullness of my father's love. I can say that even after years apart, his love is one of the greatest gifts of my life.

Gratitude Makes Room for Restoration

You see, when we make a decision to practice gratitude— even when it is not easy to do, even when things are really painful—it makes room for God to bring abundance to what feels scarce and restoration to things that feel lost!

So I made a decision to *intentionally* practice gratitude. I would take time to thank God for my father. I was so serious about this that I even cut out a picture of President Obama and his daughter Sasha hugging and laughing, because it represented the bond that I wanted to see restored in my life. I put that photo on my prayer board and over top of it I wrote: *"me and my daddy restored."* Then I put it in an area where I would see it everyday. Almost every moment I got I placed my hands on that picture and gave thanks to God for it before it came to pass.

This is when the power of gratitude came alive in our relationship. It literally changed everything for me! As I spent time with my dad, it seemed like everything that I felt like I lost in my childhood was being restored in my life as an adult. I saw restoration play out in my life with my own eyes!

Carrying His Legacy

My father has passed away now but I still think about the moments we shared. His laugh. His wisdom. His smile. His stories. Our inside jokes and conversations. This continues to give me joy. He became my best friend and he still is today. And being grateful for our time together helps me to carry our love in my heart.

I carry his legacy in the quiet, everyday moments of gratitude. Every time I stop to reflect, I cherish his memory. I know that choosing gratitude has somehow helped to heal my roots and reconnect us, just like that African proverb I mentioned earlier is teaching us to do. And my prayer is that I leave a light for those who will come after me. Same as my dad did.

Even as I am writing this journal, I cannot help but say: *Baba mi, iwọ yóò ma jẹ́ ọ̀rẹ́ mi títí láé. Mo nífẹ̀ẹ́ rẹ̀ láé láé.*

In Yoruba this means: **Daddy, you will always be my best friend. I love you forever.**

Gratitude might not erase all the pain, but it can help reveal the beauty in your life that has never dried out.

Reflection & Journal Prompt

Let us pause for a moment. Grab something to write with.

Do you have a relationship that you feel God is putting on your heart to restore? Does it still hold space in your heart? Even just a little? Take this moment to think. What is still there? Can you find one small thing to be grateful for in this relationship? Write it down.

_____

_____

_____

_____

Now, watch how even the tiniest act of gratitude can help you see something you might not have seen before.

Why is Gratitude an Important Self-care Practice for Black Women?

In America, we feel racism, sexism, and discrimination in a way that is unique. We have to deal with microaggressions, unequal pay, bias in medical care, and sometimes there is the constant pressure to prove our worth. All of this can weigh us down. On top of all that, many of us carry the weight of the Black Superwoman Trope.

The Weight of Being Black Superwoman

This is the pressure to be strong, capable, and selfless all the time. This may feel powerful at first. But it can also make it hard for us to be vulnerable or ask for help. Sometimes we push down our pain and hide our exhaustion behind a mask of perfection. Let me ask you: how many times have you been complimented on your strength when really deep down, you just want to breathe and be soft for a moment? You might be nodding your head saying, 'Yess, I do feel that way sometimes, Alease!' Listen Sis, I feel you. We have all learned how to smile and hold back our tears.

You see, when we are constantly feeling like we always have to be strong, it can sometimes lead to *high-functioning depression*. This can happen when we keep giving and pouring out nonstop, while we ignore that we are really hurting, tired, doubting ourselves, or feeling like we are not good enough.

Okay, pause here for a moment with me. Breathe. What are you feeling right now? In your body? In your thoughts? In your heart?

Sometimes we do not know that we are depressed because it does not look the way we think depression is supposed to look. It could be subtle. We may judge ourselves instead of being kind to ourselves. We might ignore our own needs, or compare ourselves to others. I have caught myself doing it too so you are not alone. But this did not start with us. This is the result of being colonized and told for hundreds of years that we were not enough.

Wounds We Carry Across the Generations

Sometimes, the message that 'we are not good enough' can come from the people who raised us, too. But let me be clear because this is not about blame. This is not about pointing fingers. The thing is, we have to recognize that our moms, grandmas, and others we love have lived through different versions of the same oppressive systems I am talking about.

nd actually, a lot of times, they can relate to the wounds we carry— often more than we know! Many of them have been through or are still going through variations of the same type of pain we ave carried. Even if they never said it out loud. So it is very possible that they interacted with us in vays that were based on their own pain. And through their fight to survive, they might not have hown the affection that we needed from them. They may have been hard on us, emotionally navailable, or even abusive. Even when they did not mean to, these things can leave an imprint on s, and make us feel like we are not good enough. It can make us feel like a burden sometimes. Unwanted. And then if we believe that we are a "burden" or "unwanted", at some point it can turn nto self-hatred or self-blame, burnout, and emptiness.

Unhealthy Coping Mechanisms

When we are hurting like this but do not feel safe to get help, we might start *self-medicating.* Or we night turn to other *coping methods* to deal with the pain in that moment. It can look like overeating vhen we are upset. Sometimes it is drinking or smoking to numb it away. Maybe it is drowning ourselves in work to avoid the pain. Or cutting ourselves off from people we care about where we tart to self-isolate. Even though these actions might help us feel better in the short term, they lead o bigger problems down the road. Like strained relationships, worsening health, unwanted habits, or deeper feelings of emptiness. I understand. We do this because we are trying to survive. But my Sister, this is not going to help us heal. You deserve to rest in a way that will heal you. You deserve a oy that is pure. You deserve a safe space to breathe and be soft for a moment.

Mind & Body Connection

Emotional pain can hurt our bodies too. If it goes on for too long it can cause inflammation, normonal imbalances, and give us a higher chance of getting sick. Even though we only make up about 10% of the U.S. population, we have much higher rates of heart disease, diabetes, death during pregnancy, and obesity than most other women.[3] These differences in health and the fact that we tend to die younger than White people make self-care even more important for our health. Taking care of yourself is not a nice-to-have. This is a basic need.

Gratitude as Self-Care

Being grateful is self-care. It will help with our mental health, physical health, and brain function. We have parts of our brains that are in charge of how we feel, that help us to remember things, and that releases serotonin and dopamine. And the thing about serotonin and dopamine is that these are chemicals that naturally help us feel good and feel happy.

Practicing gratitude has the power to ignite these parts of our brains! Where we feel happier, more at peace, and less stressed out and sad.

It can also help us move from a "fight or flight" state and calm us down. Our blood pressure goes down, our heart rate slows, and our cortisol levels drop when this happens. It makes us feel more balanced, both physically and mentally. This makes life easier and clearer.

My Sister, this is our time for taking better care of our mental health. **This is OUR season for healing!** Writing in a gratitude book is a simple but effective way to start this. And by doing this writing, we "rewire" our brains. We strengthen our neural pathways by focusing on the good things in our lives. Even if they seem small or basic. And it gets easier the more we write.

Think about a friend who checked on you recently. Or how God made something better for you. These little thoughts add up over time and will fill your cup when most needed.

Let's Check In

Gratitude Self-Care Assessment

Let's pause here and do a quick check in. Thinking about the last two weeks, how would you rate your gratitude self-care? Below are questions that will help you reflect on your current practice of gratitude and how it aligns with your self-care routine. Rate yourself on a scale of 1 to 5:

1 = Rarely or Never 2 = Sometimes 3 = Often 4 = Very Often 5 = Always

1. On most days, I pause to consider all that I'm grateful to have.

    1.   2.   3.   4.   5.

2. I keep a gratitude journal or engage in a similar practice.

    1.   2.   3.   4.   5.

3. When facing challenges, I try to look for something positive that reminds me to be thankful.

    1.   2.   3.   4.   5.

4. I express gratitude toward others by acknowledging their contributions.

    1.   2.   3.   4.   5.

5. I intentionally connect with people who nourish and support my well-being.

    1.   2.   3.   4.   5.

6. I share my gratitude with loved ones, whether through words or actions.

    1.   2.   3.   4.   5.

7. I incorporate gratitude practices that nurture my self-esteem and honor my natural beauty.

> 1.   2.   3.   4.   5.

8. I make an effort to focus on the present moment and embrace its joy.

> 1.   2.   3.   4.   5.

9. I actively seek out opportunities to mentor and uplift other Black women, when I can.

> 1.   2.   3.   4.   5.

10. I engage in creative activities that help me express my authentic self.

> 1.   2.   3.   4.   5.

Total your scores for each statement.

Scoring and Reflection:

40–50: Yassss! Sis, you're thriving! Keep nurturing what's working.

If you consistently scored high ratings with 40 or 50, then gratitude is your superpower and you are vibing in it! Your gratitude practices are reshaping and preserving your life. You are becoming stronger, more resilient, and are attracting more blessings. Yasssssss!

30–39: You're on the path, Sis!— keep showing up for yourself with love and intention.

If you consistently scored with a rating of 39 or under, pause and consider how you can incorporate more gratitude practices in your day to day life.

Below 30: A perfect moment to recommit to your self-care and lean into this journal for support.

I encourage you to come back to this assessment from time to time. Use it as a check in with yourself. Remember that practicing gratitude is part of your self-care. When you practice it on a regular basis, it can have positive effects on your overall emotional wellness and joy.

My score this month: _____ / 50

Reflections

What are your goals for how you will use this journal?

How do you see your gratitude practices boosting your emotional wellness?

_____

_____

_____

_____

_____

_____

_____

_____

_____

_____

_____

_____

_____

Be present in all things and
thankful for all things.

Maya Angelou

Sistahs Wellness Check

Sis, how are you feeling today?

Sometimes we need to hold space to identify how we are feeling, to become more self aware of our internal vibe.

If we are flooded with stress, we may disconnect emotionally and even shut down. For some, it can often feel hard to communicate what we are going through in these moments. Checking in with ourselves on a regular basis helps us with that. It makes us better at seeing our emotional patterns or triggers. Journaling about it also helps us to process our emotions and communicate them better.

When you identify where you are emotionally, take time to explore it more. Ask yourself; *'what is the situation that is impacting my internal energy'?* By doing consistent wellness checks, you can get to the bottom of why you feel what you feel.

Breathe, and let's take a moment to check in. Using the mood chart on the left, pinpoint where you are emotionally.

How are you feeling?
What is causing you to feel this? Elaborate...

Let's come back to the place throughout the week to check in. If you need extra support, feel free to scan the QR code below and I will guide you through it. It will be just like we're sitting together.

Scan to hear your guided Sistahs Wellness Check-in

Background music by SnoozyBeats via Pixabay

happy | calm

ntic | flirty | upset

ised | tired | over it

ful | pretty | discourged

trated | lonely | suspicious

cless | angry | blessed

ctive | sad | confident

Sistahs Wellness Check

Sis, how are you feeling today?

What is causing you to feel this?

_____

_____

_____

_____

_____

_____

_____

_____

_____

_____

_____

_____

_____

_____

_____

_____

_____

Reflecting on the Wins

Instead of focusing on the blessings in our lives, we sometimes place our focus on the mistakes we made in the past, on what we do not have, the setbacks that happened to us, or the situations that went wrong. While it is perfectly natural to feel a sense of sadness and grief in these circumstances, if we are not open to changing our focus, then we can become stuck in a spiral of negativity.

You see, the more we focus on a thing, the bigger that thing becomes in our perspective. Our perspective can either feed depression or feed joy. One way to break free from a negative thinking pattern is to practice a technique called *'Reflecting on the Wins.'*

Let's pause. Take a few deep breaths. Reset your focus on some of the positive things that have happened recently.

Over the past several weeks, what good news have you received?

_____

_____

_____

_____

Has someone treated you with unexpected kindness during a time when you least expected?

What was it that they did?

_____

_____

_____

_____

_____

Name a situation that turned out better than expected.

_____

_____

_____

_____

_____

Name another good thing that has happened in your life, this month.

_____

_____

_____

_____

_____

How are these experiences making your life better?

_____

_____

_____

_____

_____

Gratitude Reflections

What are you grateful for today?

_____

_____

_____

_____

_____

_____

_____

_____

_____

_____

_____

_____

_____

_____

_____

_____

_____

_____

Joy

I was listening to a podcast hosted by Iyanla Vanzant. She was speaking to a young lady who needed help and in their discussion, Iyanla offered a declaration that was both nourishing and challenging. She said, [5]"Your joy, your peace, your choices are your responsibility - regardless of what is going on…. As of today, your **joy** is your job, and you have got to work on it 8 hours a day, 40 hours a week, and your pay will be freedom!"

Take a moment to reflect on part of Iyanla's statement, *"…Your Joy is Your Job…"*

What does JOY mean to you, personally?

_____

_____

_____

_____

_____

_____

How do you nurture the joy in your life?

_____

_____

_____

_____

_____

What boundaries can you set to protect your joy?

_____

_____

_____

_____

Can you list **10** activities, situations, or objects that consistently bring you joy?

_____

_____

_____

_____

_____

_____

_____

_____

_____

_____

_____

"You is Kind.
You is Smart.
You is Important."

from the movie— The Help

Compliments

A compliment is something that we say to show that we respect and appreciate what another person is doing, wearing, or saying.

Sometimes it can feel natural to downplay the compliments that we get. It might feel as though we are not deserving of them, or maybe the attention feels embarrassing, or you might be feeling like it s too much to accept them. But giving ourselves permission to embrace compliments can actually be a form of emotional self care. When we allow ourselves to be nourished by them, it has a positive affect on our brains and our mood.

Take time to think about the compliments people have spoken over you. Look back over your text messages, emails, phone messages, and take note of the positive feedback that was delivered to you. Maybe there was a comment about how beautiful your voice is. Your personality. Your creativity. The amazing presentation you gave at work. How your skin glows. The loving spirit that you have. Your authenticity. The way that you mother your children, etc.

In the space below, write down some of the compliments that you can remember receiving in your life.

_____

_____

_____

_____

_____

_____

_____

Go back over the list of compliments that you wrote down. Next to each one, write the number of times you can remember hearing that particular compliment being spoken about you by different people.

Do you embrace the compliments that you have gotten? Explain why or why not.

_____

_____

_____

_____

_____

How can embracing those compliments, and turning them into positive affirmations that you speak over yourself, be a form of self-nourishment?

_____

_____

_____

_____

_____

_____

_____

_____

_____

Challenge: Go back again to the list of compliments that you wrote down on the previous page.

How can you turn them into a form of positive affirmations?

Use this space to turn those compliments into positive affirmations that feel authentic and uplifting.

What are you grateful for today?

_____

_____

_____

_____

_____

_____

_____

_____

_____

_____

_____

_____

_____

Grace and Mercy. ♡

Describe what 'grace' or 'mercy' means to you.

_____

_____

_____

_____

_____

From the list below, circle the situations that have happened to you in the past 12 months that you recognize as a result of grace or mercy.

New job opportunity

Dream vacation / travel

Financial Bonuses

A new business deal

Healed relationship(s)

Winning a contest

Promotion

Expunged record / Repaired reputation

Now take a moment to reflect over the past 30 days. What other moments in your life have God's grace and mercy carried you through?

_____

_____

_____

_____

_____

Okay Sis! It's testimony time! Using the space below, share a personal story where you know God showed up – a situation that could have gone wrong but didn't because of grace and mercy.

_____

_____

_____

_____

_____

_____

_____

_____

_____

How does remembering this testimony change the way you see your future, or how you see God's presence in your life?

_____

_____

_____

_____

_____

_____

_____

_____

_____

_____

_____

_____

_____

_____

Gratitude Affirmation

I am learning to see the goodness in my life more and more.

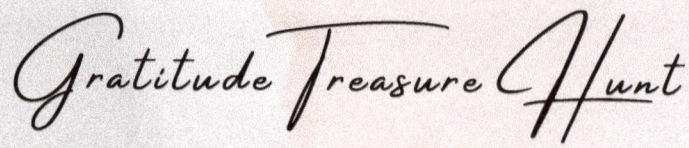

Gratitude Treasure Hunt

Take a deep breathe in. Hold. Breathe out. Pause.

Look around you. Pay attention to the sights, sounds, scenes, textures, and flavors right there where you are. Share how each thing you see has been a blessing to you. Once completed, set aside a few minutes each week to revisit this list and reflect on any new feelings that come up.

☐ find a piece of artwork in your home, office, or on your cell phone that makes you feel warm in your heart. Describe why this piece is special to you.

_____

_____

_____

☐ Think of an item in your kitchen, bedroom, living room, or dining room that feeds your joy. Use the space below to describe it.

_____

_____

_____

☐ Identify a book, movie, or tv show in your home that inspires you. What is your favorite chapter or line from it?

_____

_____

☐ Is there an email, card, or text message from someone who has expressed their gratitude towards you? Who is it from? What did they say?

_____

_____

How do these sentimental items remind you to be grateful?

_____

_____

_____

_____

_____

_____

How can you show your appreciation for these blessings?

_____

_____

_____

_____

_____

_____

_____

Gratitude Reflections

What are you grateful for today?

_____

_____

_____

_____

_____

_____

_____

_____

_____

_____

_____

_____

_____

_____

_____

Celebrate Your Sistahs

Think of your Sistahs — all of the women in your life.

Is there a woman in your life who recently had a win, reached a goal, or stepped into something beautiful — even if it stirred mixed feelings in you?

_____

_____

_____

What might it feel like to genuinely celebrate her joy?

_____

_____

_____

How could celebrating her success — with her — make your life better?

_____

_____

_____

How does her success story inspire and encourage you?

_____

_____

_____

_____

_____

_____

What is one thing you can do to celebrate and uplift her?

_____

_____

_____

_____

Challenge: Share your joy with the woman you identified above. Send her a kind note or a text from your heart. Let her know how proud and happy you are of her and share how she has inspired you.

I appreciate the laughter and joy that fill my life, reminding me of the happiness that is blessing me.

Big Belly Laughin'

Did you know that even science backs up the benefits of humor? According to health psychologist Dr. Grace Tworek[6] from the Cleveland Clinic, laughter can be as powerful as medicine. Here's why:

- Laughter reduces anxiety and stress.
- It builds positive relationships.
- It reduces brain fog.
- It boosts your heart health.

Think of a time that you laughed so hard that your stomach started to hurt.

_____

_____

_____

_____

How do you feel after you let out a good laugh?

_____

_____

_____

_____

What are your top 3 favorite TV shows and/or movies that you can re-watch that will always have you cracking up into big belly laughter?

_____

_____

_____

_____

_____

How can you bring more laughter into your life?

_____

_____

_____

_____

How can finding more ways to laugh everyday help you feel better?

_____

_____

_____

_____

Challenge: Share one of your favorite television shows, movies, moments with a loved one to spread joy. *Closing Thought* – **Laughter is medicine.** It helps us find joy even in the little things. Give yourself permission to laugh more. Share a funny story. Watch your favorite show. Your laugh can help you heal.

Gratitude Reflections

What are you grateful for today?

Gratitude Affirmation

I embrace my gentleness, softness, and vulnerability.

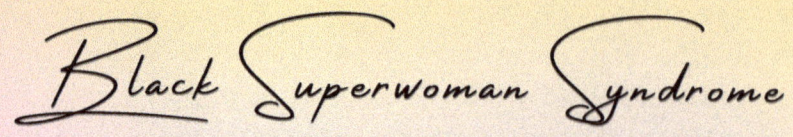

Queen, You Cannot Pour from an Empty Cup

As Black women, we sometimes struggle with a phenomenon called the Black Superwoman Syndrome[7]. This is a schema that many of us have internalized that is traced back to colonization, historical oppression and systemic racism.

Many of us are stressed out because we are often expected to proverbially 'hold it down', be strong, and take care of everyone else, even at the expense of our own emotional wellness. Yet when we are tired, down, sad, lonely, or depressed, who is 'holding it down' for us?

The thing is, **you matter too.** Without creating the space to care for our mental and emotional health, we become more at risk to various forms of psychological distress such as anxiety and depression. World famous author and expert on self care, Eleanor Brownn, makes it plain for us. "Rest and self care are so important. When you take time to replenish your spirit, it allows you to serve others from the overflow. You cannot serve from an empty vessel."

What does being strong mean to you personally? Does being strong always mean pushing through? Or can it also mean allowing yourself to rest and receive support?

_____

_____

_____

_____

_____

This pressure can weigh us down. Let us unpack why it is okay to let go of that weight.

Where, in your life, do you feel the pressure to be strong?

_____

_____

_____

_____

Psalms 23[8] reminds us that it is okay for us to rest, and that it is God's will for our cup to overflow. How can you give yourself permission to rest, and allow your cup to overflow with what God has for you?

_____

_____

_____

_____

_____

_____

Imagine living in that space of rest and softness with God. What feels different? What do you feel most grateful for in this moment?

_____

_____

_____

_____

The concept of the "Black Superwoman Schema"[7] is rooted in the scholarly work of Dr. Cheryl Woods-Giscombe'. Her research highlights the psychological and emotional implications of this phenomenon among Black women.

Gratitude Reflections

Take a deep breath in. Hold for 5 counts. Breathe out.
Pause.

What were the 3 best moments about today?

_____

_____

_____

_____

_____

_____

_____

_____

_____

_____

_____

_____

Brown Skin

Queen, you are beautiful. Your brown skin is beautiful. You are uniquely created with an abundance of melanin that gives you that glowingly royal hue. Yet, we know that having a brown complexion can come with its challenges in this society.

We are not always treated fairly. Snap judgments are sometimes made about us simply based on our hue. It might come in the form of demeaning, insulting, or offensive behaviors—whether from people who are of well-intention or otherwise. If we internalize this, it could dampen our sense of worth.

Today, I stand with you in solidarity to resist any and all forms of negative messaging.

Your brown skin is beautiful.

BROWN SKIN Affirmation Challenge

Using each letter in the words **BROWN SKIN**, describe 9 things you love and cherish about yourself as a beautiful Brown-Skinned woman.

Letter	What I Love About Myself
B	
R	
O	
W	
N	
S	
K	
I	
N	

Take a moment to think about how it feels to write these truths about yourself. What do these qualities show you about your inner beauty, talents, and self-worth?

Self-Compassion

"The Lord is close to the brokenhearted and saves those who are crushed in spirit."
(Psalms 34:18 NIV)[8]

Self-compassion means treating yourself with the same kindness, care, and understanding that you would offer to a dear friend in a difficult moment. Some of us have moments where we are hard on ourselves. And sometimes we can hold ourselves to really high standards that can be unrealistic. We might be looking back and remembering a situation that we wished we handled better. Or maybe we secretly expected to be further along in life. Sometimes it is a small thing, but sometimes it is not. Maybe it was something that happened today, this month, this year, or even at a different time in your life, but for some reason it is coming up for you right now.

Before you start writing, take a deep breath …hold… and breathe out.

Now, when you think about that situation, what feelings come up?

_____

_____

_____

_____

_____

_____

_____

Now, imagine your really close friend came to you sharing these same feelings.
What words would you say to encourage her?
How would you remind her about her worth and the love that surrounds her?

_____

_____

_____

_____

_____

Now, read back what you wrote. What if these words were meant for you, too?
Slowly re-read it to yourself. Stay right here for a moment. Let the words sink in.

How does it feel to speak this affirmation over you?

_____

_____

_____

What is **one word** that you can take with you today that will remind you to show yourself
grace?

Here are a few examples to choose from:

Growing	Whole	Restored	Valuable
Peace	Enough	Light	Precious
Safe	Covered	Loved	Cared For
	Gentle	Worthy	

Write your word here:

_____

$\mathcal{L}ooking \; \mathcal{B}ack$

Sometimes it is a healthy practice to look back and remember how far you have come from and to hold space to appreciate God's hand at work in your life. If you have a camera roll on your phone, have a social media account with photos with special moments, or even have pictures in your home on the wall or photo album– take a moment to visit those photos.

Look over your pictures. Write down any blessings that stand out to you, no matter how big or small.

Where are you in the picture you see? What did you get to do or experience?

_____

_____

_____

_____

How does that photo capture a moment where you felt happy, blessed, or loved?

_____

_____

_____

_____

_____

_____

_____

Think about how this picture shows God's faithfulness in your life.

_____

_____

_____

_____

_____

_____

_____

If there is anything else you cherish about the memory in this photo – write it here.

_____

_____

_____

_____

_____

_____

_____

_____

Restored. Repaired. Healed.

"He restores my soul; He leads me in the paths of righteousness for His name's sake."
(Psalms 23:3 NKJV)[8]

Have you ever had a situation in your life that was restored, repaired, or healed?

Thinking about the last 12 months, write about a situation that God has turned around for you.

_____

_____

_____

_____

_____

_____

How did this situation grow your faith?

_____

_____

_____

_____

_____

What lessons did you learn from this experience?

_____

_____

_____

_____

_____

_____

_____

_____

How has this restoration impacted the way you trust in God, or how you see your life?

_____

_____

_____

_____

_____

_____

Challenge: Take a moment to give thanks to God for what has been restored, repaired, and healed! How can you use this experience to encourage someone?

Reframing Regrets

Turning Regret Into Redemption

Maybe there was a missed opportunity. Lost time. A mistake. Something you did. Something you did not do. If you are feeling regret, hear me out: **you are not alone**.

Many people experience this pain. Oftentimes, we can be prone to self-medicate in order to cope. Sometimes we dwell on those regrets without moving forward, which can lead to feelings of helplessness and negativity. Practicing gratefulness can be a strategy to help to set us free from feeling stuck in this.

The first step is a courageous one — to embrace the pain of regret.

Can you think of a situation where you experienced regret?

How did you respond and what did you learn from this experience?

_____

_____

_____

_____

If you have done something that hurt yourself or someone else, what would it look like to make amends for that? If you feel like you have missed an opportunity or made a mistake, how do you see redemption showing up in your life?

_____

_____

_____

_____

challenge you to take a compassionate look back at this situation. Look at everything that was at play at the time. The circumstances. The environment. Who you were then. Maybe there are things you did not know at that time, that you know now.

How can you give yourself grace?

_____

_____

_____

_____

_____

_____

_____

What is one small action you can take today to step into the woman that God has called you to be?

_____

_____

_____

_____

_____

_____

_____

_____

Turning Regret Into Redemption

God specializes in turning situations around. Mistakes can be turned into miracles. Regret can be healed and restoration can come. Healing, wholeness, and deliverance is possible for you. **Use the space below to discuss any regrets with God. Turn the issue over to God.**

_____

_____

_____

_____

_____

_____

Use the space below to offer gratitude to God in advance for bringing miracles, healing, delivering and grace in this situation.

_____

_____

_____

_____

_____

_____

_____

_____

_____

_____

_____

_____

_____

Use this space to write a personal affirmation over yourself.

_____

_____

_____

_____

_____

_____

_____

Closing Thought: Regret does not define you. God can bring beauty from ashes. Sis, repeat after me: "Today, I am moving forward with power, peace, and restoration."

"It was when I realized I needed to stop trying to be somebody else and be myself, I actually started to own, accept and love what I had."

Tracee Ellis Ross

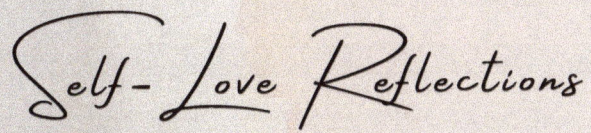

Self-Love Reflections

What are 3 things about your body that you are grateful for?

_____

_____

_____

_____

Hold space to appreciate how hard your body works and shows up for you.
Take a moment to reflect:

What has your body carried you through?

What does your body allow you to do that brings you joy or fulfillment?

_____

_____

_____

_____

What is one small act of self-care you can do today to show your body some love?

_____

_____

Gratitude Reflections

What are you grateful for today?

_____

_____

_____

_____

_____

_____

_____

_____

_____

_____

_____

_____

_____

_____

_____

_____

I Woke up Like This

Take notice of the ways that your natural beauty is glowing this morning.

Use the space below to appreciate how your beauty naturally shows up for you.

_____

_____

_____

_____

_____

_____

_____

_____

_____

_____

_____

_____

_____

'*Thank you*' is the best prayer
that anyone could say.
I say that one a lot.
Thank you expresses extreme
gratitude, humility,
understanding.

Alice Walker

Thank You Lord!

Take a moment to think about how God has been present in your life.

How has God answered your prayers?

Use the space below to reflect on specific ways God has shown up for you. Big or small.

_____

_____

_____

_____

_____

How is God blessing you right now? Think about the blessings you are experiencing today — spiritual, emotional, physical, or material—and write about them below.

_____

_____

_____

_____

_____

_____

_____

_____

_____

_____

_____

_____

_____

Take time to give thanks for God's faithfulness, love, and provision. Write a prayer of gratitude below.

_____

_____

_____

_____

_____

_____

_____

_____

_____

_____

_____

_____

Thank You for Being There

Think about the last two weeks. Was there one person who has showed up for you — maybe through a phone call, a text, a kind word, or even just by being present?

Who immediately comes to mind?

_____

_____

_____

How did they leave you feeling inspired, encouraged, or seen?

_____

_____

_____

If you're not sure where to start, try completing the following sentences to help you flesh out your thoughts:

"I'll never forget that time when you..."

_____

_____

_____

_____

_____

_____

_____

_____

"When I felt forgotten, you showed up by..."

_____

_____

_____

"Your words that day reminded me..."

_____

_____

_____

"Because of you, I believed again in..."

_____

_____

_____

_____

_____

_____

_____

How does it feel to name the way they supported you?

_____

_____

_____

_____

_____

_____

_____

If you wanted to honor or celebrate their support, what might that look like?

_____

_____

_____

_____

_____

_____

_____

Gratitude Reflections

What are you grateful for today?

"...It is more blessed to give than to receive."

Acts 20:35 [8]

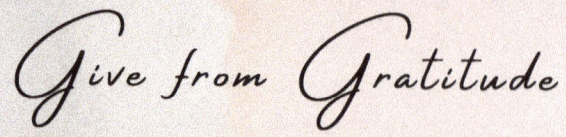

Blessing Others with What You Have

Giving and being grateful go hand in hand. According to Karns[9], giving from a place of gratitude helps us to turn our attention to others and see the joy in interacting with them. It invites us to step into a space of generosity and purpose, where we can use our blessings to make a positive impact.

Being generous has a positive effect on our brains—it makes us feel happier and more fulfilled.

When you give from a place of gratitude, you not only help other people, but you also level up your own sense of purpose. Sometimes, the chance to bless someone else starts with making a list of all the good things we already have. What do you have? This can be our time, our love, our resources, or even our words of support. For this project, let's look at **what's in your closet** as a real-life example of this idea.

Start with Gratitude

Being grateful means recognizing what we have, no matter how little or how much. **As you look through your closet, what items are you grateful to have?**

_____

_____

Are there any you no longer wear or use that could bless someone else?

_____

_____

_____

_____

_____

Sharing Your Blessings

Who would be blessed by the things you want to give? Think of a woman in your community or someone in your family who would be encouraged by the items you no longer need. Maybe there is an organization that could benefit from an item you do not use anymore. Write down their names. Write down the organizations. Write down the items you want to donate:

A Lady / Organization I'm Thinking of   **Item(s) I Want to Give**

_____

_____

_____

_____

_____

_____

_____

_____

_____

_____

_____

Make it a Plan
- Sort and gather the items you are ready to give.
- Reach out to the women or organizations that you have written down. Schedule a time to drop off those things.

Closing Thought: Giving, especially from a place of gratitude, blesses other people. But it also fills your heart with joy and purpose. When you give —whether it is your time, resources, or love—you create a ripple effect of kindness. Let your generosity show the gratitude in your heart. And trust that what you give will come back to you in ways you cannot imagine. ♥

Gratitude Reflections

What is one thing or who is one person that you have in your life in this moment, that you did not have a week ago, a month ago, or a year ago?

_____

_____

_____

_____

_____

_____

_____

How has this blessing impacted your life?

_____

_____

_____

_____

_____

_____

Gratitude Reflections

What are you grateful for today?

_____

_____

_____

_____

_____

_____

_____

_____

_____

_____

_____

_____

_____

_____

Gratitude Affirmation

I am blessed to be
surrounded by my
girlfriends.

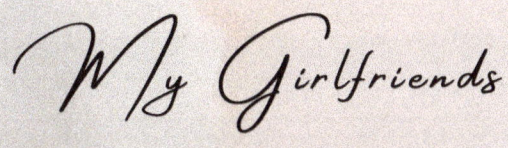 

My Girlfriends

The Gift of Sisterhood

How are your girlfriends blessing your life?

Think of the friends in your life who show up for you. These are the Sistahs who not only support you, but also challenge you to be better. They always have your back no matter what.

List each of their names one by one.

Next to her name, write one quality that you deeply admire about her..

My Girlfriend(s)   **One Thing I Admire about Her**

_____

_____

_____

_____

_____

_____

_____

_____

_____

Why does that quality matter to you?

How has their friendship helped to shape, support, and bless your life?

_____

_____

_____

_____

_____

_____

_____

_____

_____

_____

_____

_____

Challenge: If you can, tell one of your friends what you wrote.

So Glad I Made It!

Think about a situation that you have walked through, and use the space below to discuss the moment where you saw God showing up in that situation.

_____

_____

_____

_____

_____

_____

What have you learned to cherish about God, yourself, and your loved ones since this experience?

_____

_____

_____

_____

_____

_____

_____

Who have you grown closer to as a result of going through this situation?

_____

_____

_____

_____

_____

_____

_____

How did the adversity that you went through, prepare you for a greater purpose or calling?

_____

_____

_____

_____

_____

_____

_____

_____

Gratitude Reflections

What are you grateful for today?

_____

_____

_____

_____

_____

_____

_____

_____

_____

_____

_____

_____

_____

_____

_____

_____

Making a Love List

Do you have a '***Love List***'? I am talking about a list of hobbies or activities that feeds your joy. Having a hobby can be a form of self-care when they enhance your mental, emotional, or spiritual health. Below, here is a list of activities to get you started.

Circle the ones that you love.

Taking a hot bubble bath

Taking care of your plants

Getting your favorite cup of coffee

Quiet time with God

Going to the bookstore

Listening to Music (Jazz, R&B, Gospel, Neo Soul, etc)

Going for walks in nature

Shopping

Spending time with your girls

A nice hot cup of tea

Taking a nap

Gardening

Going to the theatre

Going dancing

Watching your favorite tv shows

Getting your nails or toes done

Reading a good book

Are there any hobbies you love to do that are not listed on the previous page?

_____

_____

_____

_____

Which hobby is your most favorite? Why?

_____

_____

_____

How does that hobby(ies) bring you more joy?

_____

_____

_____

_____

_____

_____

_____

Gratitude Mantras

"Let the words of my mouth and the meditation of my heart be acceptable in your sight, O Lord." (Psalm 19:14 KJV)[8]

Words have power.

What you say to yourself and about yourself matters. A mantra is a basic word or phrase that we repeat to ourselves, that resets our focus. Here is an example of how to make a gratitude mantra:

- Say **Why** You are Grateful: When you say what you are grateful for, unpack the reason why. For example, if you say "I am grateful for my daughter", write down the reason why and be specific. Here is an example of how you might do that: *"I am grateful for my daughter because when she confides in me, I feel more connected to her."*

- **Feel** the Emotion after Your Why: After you say why you are grateful, stay with that feeling. Do not rush. Hold space to feel that emotion in your body. Savor it!

Let's practice! Using the template below, make your personal gratitude mantra by filling in the blank:

I am grateful for... _____

_____

_____

because... _____

_____

_____

and I feel... _____

_____

_____

Create Your Own Mantras!

Use the space below to create your own your personal gratitude mantras:

_____

_____

_____

_____

_____

_____

_____

_____

_____

_____

_____

_____

_____

_____

_____

_____

Music that Heals the Soul

Music has been a staple in our community for centuries. It was one of the superpowers of our ancestors. We have used music as a creative outlet to get us through slavery, Jim Crow, the Civil Rights Movement, institutional racism, and the unique challenges we face as Black women.

We use it as a vehicle to worship, emotionally process, recharge, refocus, and create a vibe for celebration, culture, and uplifting.

Did you know that music is also scientifically proven to be therapeutic? Mental health experts Kendra Cherry and Steven Gans[10] say that listening to music can help us deal with anxiety and depression, and improve our mood right away. This truth is close to home for me because music is often what I turn to when I need to change my mood or remember to be thankful.

I love all types of music, but there are certain songs that really help me think about the good things that have happened in my life. These songs give me joy. *"Happy"* by Tasha Cobbs Leonard is at the top of my list. This joint right here makes me feel lighter no matter what kind of day I am having. It brings my attention back to the happiness that comes from knowing that God loves and takes care of me.

Another favorite is *"Blessings on Blessings"* by Anthony Brown & Group Therapy. It makes me want to speak life over myself and my situation. Sometimes it helps me remember to be thankful for all the good things in my life, no matter how big or small they feel.

My Gratitude Playlist

Inspired by **Moments of Gratitude for Black Women** (Apple Music/ iTunes)

These 10 songs that you see listed below always put me in a positive mood and make me feel grateful for my life, and the people I love. You can listen to **My Gratitude Playlist** exclusively on Apple Music.

If you are an iPhone user, just scan the QR code below, and let the music uplift your spirit. If you do not have access to Apple Music, feel free to use the song list below to build your own on another platform, like Spotify or YouTube. Before you scan and listen, let's take this moment to reflect. What type of music has lifted you out of a low moment or reminded you of God's faithfulness?

Note: Playlist currently available exclusively on iTunes/ Apple Music.

My Gratitude Playlist

Happy (Live) – Tasha Cobbs Leonard
Blessings on Blessings – Anthony Brown & group therAPy
In the Morning – Mary Mary
Golden - Jill Scott
We're Blessed – Fred Hammond
You Are Worthy – J.J. Hairston & Youthful Praise
Thank You – Mary Mary
Won't He Do It – Koryn Hawthorne
I Gotta Believe – Yolanda Adams
Gotta Believe – Tasha Cobbs Leonard
Bonus Goodness of God - CeCe Winans

With these songs as a guide, you can start your day with joy. Let the words to these songs make you feel better and help you think about your blessings.

Your Gratitude Playlist

Now I want you to think about the type of music that make you feel happy.

What kind of music do you like? What songs make you think of all the good things in your life?

Is there a song that makes you feel lighter? How about a song that makes you feel grateful for someone or something?

- What song makes you smile?
- What feelings come up when you hear it?

Write down 10 songs you could put on Your Gratitude Playlist to remind you about the good things in your life:

1. _____

2. _____

3. _____

4. _____

5. _____

6. _____

7. _____

8. _____

9. _____

10. _____

Closing Thought: Keep your "Gratitude Playlist" close by and listen to it whenever you want to feel better. Music is a gift that can remind you of how beautiful life is. Think of all the good things in your life while you listen to it.

Goodness

The word for the day is "goodness"

What does that word mean to you, personally?

_____

_____

_____

_____

Take a moment to write down good qualities about yourself.

_____

_____

_____

_____

Think of someone who you admire. Reflect on their good qualities and list them below.

_____

_____

_____

_____

hink of someone in your life who has been difficult to work with. Take a moment to point out the good qualities in that person. Try to fill this section with as many positive traits as you can.

_____

_____

_____

_____

_____

_____

_____

_____

How does recognizing the goodness in this person help you approach them with more understanding or compassion? Take a moment to write your thoughts below:

_____

_____

_____

_____

_____

_____

_____

_____

_____

Gratitude Word Search

Puzzles have a way of refocusing our minds. They help us slow down. To reflect. And they help us to feel a sense of accomplishment. On this crossword puzzle, circle or highlight as many words you can find. If a certain word speaks to your heart, take time to reflect on why. Feel free to journal about it on the next page.

h	h	z	a	d	w	f	a	m	i	l	y	k	q	u
o	o	b	e	a	u	t	y	v	m	l	f	j	u	n
x	p	p	l	i	w	g	g	k	g	i	s	n	i	i
h	p	p	e	e	i	x	r	r	g	n	n	d	e	q
s	o	s	p	r	s	u	a	p	i	s	k	n	t	u
e	r	u	l	r	o	s	c	e	g	p	f	e	t	e
l	t	p	g	o	y	x	e	a	t	j	x	s	j	n
c	u	p	f	a	v	o	r	c	q	r	f	s	m	e
a	n	o	f	r	q	e	j	e	g	e	j	t	e	s
r	i	r	d	e	s	u	c	c	e	s	s	y	s	s
i	t	t	n	r	e	w	o	p	r	e	p	u	s	n
m	y	a	g	o	o	d	n	e	s	s	g	h	j	g

key:

bless. grace. opportunity. uniqueness. goodness. joy. inspire. gifts. favor. my girls. beauty. miracles. hope. quiet time. peace. superpower. success. kindness. support. family. love.

Word Search Reflections - Your Word for the Day

Now that you have completed the word search, which word(s) stood out to you the most?

_____

_____

_____

Why does this word feel important to you right now?

_____

_____

_____

_____

_____

What word from the search will you carry with you as your 'Word for the Day'?

_____

_____

What affirmation can you write using this word?

_____

_____

How will you let this word guide you today?

_____

_____

What are you grateful for today?

_____

_____

_____

_____

_____

_____

_____

_____

_____

_____

_____

_____

_____

_____

_____

_____

Work in Progress

As you reflect on your day, think about the progress you made thus far.

What milestones have you accomplished today?

_____

_____

_____

_____

_____

_____

Now, think about the milestones (or goals) that you have accomplished in the last 12 months. Name at least 5 accomplishments.

_____

_____

_____

_____

_____

_____

_____

What is it like to see how far you have come?

"To describe my mother would be to write about a hurricane in its perfect power. Or the climbing, falling colors of a rainbow."

Maya Angelou

Healing the Mother Wound

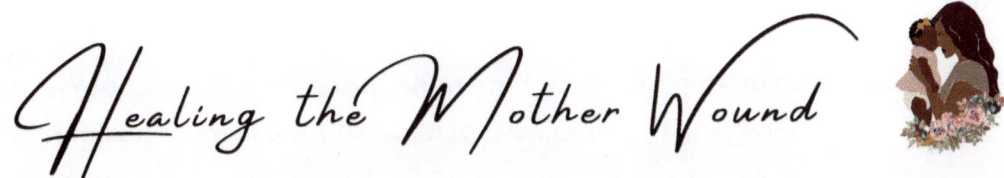

nother wound is a deep pain that can start when a child is young. Sometimes it is because the other is still dealing with her own emotional wounds. Or because she does not have enough help, she cannot fully care for her child's feelings.

is hurt can make us feel like we are forgotten, not good enough, or not worthy. And this can ke it hard for us to make healthy connections with other people. A lot of times, this wound is passed down through families and it is shaped by all of the pain that our mothers and grandmothers went through.

It takes time to heal this wound, but it is possible. It is possible to grow and improve our relationships with others and ourselves if we take care of our emotions and love ourselves.

My sister, have you been wounded in this way? Breathe. Tell me what happened...

_____

_____

_____

_____

_____

_____

_____

_____

_____

_____

_____

Sis, I want you to pause right here to breathe. Breathe out. Breathe again. Your breath work is cleansing. And it ushers in healing.

Give yourself permission! Permission to accept the pain. To feel disappointment. To griev the loss of what you expected to get but did not. This is a big step toward healing. Do not ignore or suppress it!

Use the space below to share how you are feeling right now.

_____

_____

_____

_____

_____

_____

_____

_____

_____

_____

_____

_____

Reconnecting with Your Inner Child

You were not the one who caused this pain.
But you can be the one to help it heal.

Take this time to imagine the little girl who lives inside of you. Ask her:

- What do you need from me right now?

- What are you feeling?

_____

_____

_____

**See yourself sitting with her. Make room for her feelings. Tell her the things
she always needed to hear. Write it here:**

_____

_____

_____

_____

_____

_____

_____

_____

**Pause. Breathe deep. Breathe out. Breathe again.
Repeat the breaths.**

Thinking about Your Mother

What does forgiving your mother look like for you? Take your time with this. Forgiveness is personal. It does not look the same for everybody.

_____

_____

_____

_____

_____

What can you do to become more aware of the good things you got from your mother?

_____

_____

_____

_____

How can you honor all of what she did—or tried to do—for you?

_____

_____

_____

_____

lot of us may have had painful, distant, or even absent relationships with our mothers. If it is too much for you to think about her right now: **I understand**. It can be hard when we have been hurt so deeply. So feel free to pause if you need to. And when you are ready, come back. And we will try again together.

Gratitude can take different forms. Is there something she taught you? Through her actions, her struggles, or even her absence? **In the space below, write down any gratitude you have for your mother, the lessons you have learned, or the experiences that helped you grow:**

_____

_____

_____

_____

_____

Recognizing Other Mother Figures

Think about a motherly-figure who has been there for you and helped shape you.

What is her name?
When did she become a part of your life?
How did she influence you?

_____

_____

_____

_____

Think about specific events that happened to you along the way and how they helped you grow.

_____

_____

_____

_____

_____

What would you say if you could tell her how you feel about how she changed your life?

_____

_____

_____

_____

_____

_____

_____

If it feels right for you, think about how you could thank your mother or maternal figure for the things she has done to make your life better. This could be done by calling her, sending a card, or even having a quiet thought in her honor.

Closing Thought

Healing from the Mother Wound takes time. Be kind to yourself and it is okay to be honest about what you feel. As you go through this, love on your younger self. With God, any pain that has been passed down through generations can be turned into love and growth.

Hope Again. Dream Again.

Sometimes in life it can be hard to feel hopeful. Sis, if you are feeling this way, you are not alone. **Use the space below to share how you feel**.

_____

_____

_____

_____

_____

_____

_____

"For I know the thoughts that I think toward you, says the Lord, thoughts of peace and not of evil, to give you a future and a hope." (Jeremiah 29:11 NKJV)[8]

Even when it looks and feels like there is no hope, God can give you hope.
How can you open your heart to the hope that God is giving to you in this season?

_____

_____

_____

_____

_____

_____

_____

_____

Whose story can you pull from to find the encouragement you need when it feels as though there is no hope? This could be a story from the Bible. A loved one. A person you never met – but you heard their story and never forgot it. Or maybe...it could be your own story! **Write about the story that is speaking to your heart right now.**

_____

_____

_____

_____

_____

_____

What is another method that has worked for you in the past, that helped to restore your hope?

_____

_____

_____

_____

_____

_____

_____

Closing Thought: Feel free to pray. Or go back to a page in this book that speaks to you. God loves you and He is working behind the scenes for you. Even when you cannot see that. Sis, I promise that better times are on the way. **You are not forgotten**.

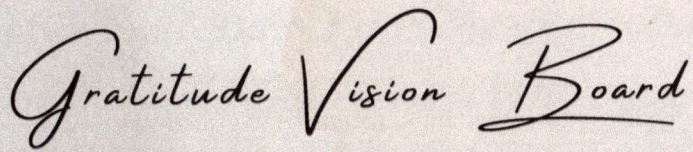

How to Create Your Gratitude Vision Board

Okay, it's time to grab some cardboard, paper, scissors, magazines, tape, and your creativity. We're about to create a **Gratitude Vision Board!**

Your Gratitude Vision Board is a visual reminder of how you have been blessed. I encourage you to use it as a way to express your faith in God. Think of it as your personal space for creativity, reflection, and joy—a reminder of the goodness already in your life and the hope that's on its way.

What You'll Need
Gather anything else that helps you get creative. Here are a few ideas:

Pictures of people, places, or things that make you happy

Thank-you notes, cards, or scriptures

Magazine cuttings that give you inspiration

Words or statements that represent how you have been blessed

Words or statements that represent your intentions for the future

Where to Place Your Board
Find a spot where your vision board will encourage you each day. Here are a few ideas:

Bedroom: to help you feel refreshed every morning

Desk: to help you feel grounded all day

Cell Phone: on the home screen as a quick way to refocus

Prayer Closet: to help you reconnect with your faith

Look at it as much as you can. Let it inspire you. Let it strengthen your faith.

Reflections as You Create Your Board

Before you start, think about these questions below:

What are 5 things you're thankful for right now?

_____

_____

_____

_____

_____

What are 5 things your heart is open to receiving in this season?

_____

_____

_____

_____

_____

What affirmations, quotes, or images represent the blessings you already have, and the new ones you are ready to welcome?

_____

_____

_____

_____

My Gratitude Vision Board

Here is an example of a Gratitude Vision Board I designed. Now it's your turn. Feel free to use this as an example as you start putting yours together. I know it is going to be beautiful!

Closing Thought: Take your time making your Gratitude Vision Board. It is a personal project and there is no right or wrong way to create one. When you are done, pray over you board and thank God for what He has already done – and still doing. Then make it your daily reminder to celebrate the blessings in your life and to trust God for what He is about to do.

Gratitude Reflections

Take a deep breath in. Hold it for 5 counts. Breathe out. Pause. Repeat 2 more times.

Open your hands.

Reflect on the good things you have experienced within the last 24 hours.

Visualize seeing each of those good things being handed to you, one by one.

Express gratitude to God for each good thing by calling them out by name.

List each one below.

_____

_____

_____

_____

_____

_____

_____

_____

_____

Gratitude Reflections

What is one thing that brought you rest this week?

_____

_____

_____

_____

How did it make your life better?

_____

_____

_____

_____

_____

How can a moment of rest strengthen your relationship with God?

_____

_____

_____

_____

_____

_____

How can you make rest a regular part of your routine?

_____

_____

_____

_____

How is God inviting you to slow down and rest right now?

_____

_____

_____

_____

How does resting help you to reconnect with who you really are?

_____

_____

_____

_____

_____

Gratitude Reflections

Is there a blessing in your life that you are overlooking?

_____

_____

_____

_____

_____

_____

_____

_____

_____

_____

_____

_____

_____

_____

_____

Gratitude Reflections

What are you grateful for today?

_____

_____

_____

_____

_____

_____

_____

_____

_____

_____

_____

_____

_____

_____

_____

_____

Resources

Mental Health Resources for Black Women

Therapy for Black Girls	https://providers.therapyforblackgirls.com
Melanin & Mental Health	https://www.melaninandmentalhealth.com
Inclusive Therapists ♥	https://www.inclusivetherapists.com
Clinicians of Color	https://www.cliniciansofcolor.org
Psychology Today	https://www.psychologytoday.com

Stories and Affirmations that Uplift

Affirmations for Black Women A Journal – Oludara Adeeyo

Self-Care for Black Women – Oludara Adeeyo

Black Joy – Tracey Michae'l Lewis-Giggetts

All Hope is Found – Sarah Jakes Roberts

The Nap Ministry: Rest as Resistance – Tricia Hersey

Life, I Swear: Intimate Stories from Black Women on Identity, Healing, and Self-Trust – Chloe Dulce Louvouezo

Sisterhood Heals: The Transformative Power of Healing in Community – Joy Harden Bradford, PhD.

Seen, Loved and Heard: A Guided Journal for Feeding the Soul – Tabitha Brown

YouTube Channels for Emotional Wellness

Melanated Affirmations

The Nap Ministry

Dr. Anita Phillips

Resources

Podcasts for Inspiration and Conversation

Black Girls Heal
She's So Lucky The Podcast
Woman Evolve
Therapy for Black Girls The Podcast
You Need To Hear This

Meditation and Mindfulness Resources

Black Girls Breathing	https://blackgirlsbreathing.com/
The Calm App	www.calm.com
The Abide App	www.abide.com
The Exhale App	www.exhale-app.com

Please note: The resources that are listed in this section are shared solely for general guidance. For personalized and professional care, please consult with a licensed mental health professional.
My Sister, this is our season for healing 🤎

Bibliography

1. Merriam-Webster. (2022). Merriam-Webster's Collegiate Dictionary (11th ed.). Merriam-Webster.

2. Harden-Bradford, J., Ph.D. (2020). The mental wellness benefits of practicing gratitude. Therapy for Black Girls.

3. Chinn, J. J., Martin, I. K., & Redmond, N. (2002). Health equity among Black women in the United States. Journal of Women's Health, 30(2), 212-219. https://doi.org/10.1089/jwh.2020.8868.

4. Warren, Alease (2024). Modified Gratitude Assessment Prompt. Based on the original work by OpenAI. https://openai.com/gratitude-assessment-prompt/. Accessed January 30, 2024 .

5. Vanzant, I. (2023, January 18). Your joy is your job. In The R Spot with Iyanla. iHeartMedia, Inc. https://www.iheart.com/podcast/the-r-spot-with-iyanla.

6. Cleveland Clinic Health Essentials. (2022). Why laughing is good for you. Mental Health. Retrieved from https://health.clevelandclinic.org/is-laughing-good-for-you/.

7. Woods-Giscombé, C. L. (2010). Superwoman schema: African American women's views on stress, strength, and health. Qualitative Health Research, 20(5), 668-683.

8. New King James Bible. (1982). Holy Bible, New King James Version. Thomas Nelson. (Original work published 1982).

9. Karns, C. (2017). Why a grateful brain is a giving one. Greater Good Magazine. Retrieved from https://greatergood.berkeley.edu/article/item/why_a_grateful_brain_is_a_giving_one.

10. Cherry, K., MSEd, & Gans, S., MD. (2022). How listening to music can have psychological benefits. Verywell Mind. Retrieved from https://www.verywellmind.com/surprising-psychological-benefits-of-music-4126866.

Bibliography

Angelou, M. (n.d.). To describe my mother would be to write about a hurricane in its perfect power. Or the climbing, falling colors of a rainbow. Goodreads. Retrieved from https://www.goodreads.com/quotes/13397

Moments of Gratitude for Black Women. Apple Music, 2024, https://music.apple.com/. Accessed 26 June 2025.

Ross, T. E. (n.d.). It was when I realized I needed to stop trying to be somebody else and be myself, I actually started to own, accept and love what I had. herNetwork. Retrieved from https://https://www.hernetwork.co/5-empowering-statements-by-tracee-ellis-ross/.

Taylor, T. (2011). The Help. DreamWorks Pictures; Reliance Entertainment; Participant Media; Image Nation; 1492 Pictures; Harbinger Pictures.

Walker, A. (2015, March 15). Interview by J. Smith. The Power of Gratitude. Oprah Magazine. Retrieved from https://www.oprah.com/alice-walker-interview.